Matthew Stroshane

About the Author

MARK DOTY's seven books of poems and three books of nonfiction prose have been honored by the National Book Critics Circle Award, the PEN/Martha Albrand Prize for First Nonfiction, the Los Angeles Times Book Prize, a Whiting Writers' Award, a Lila Wallace–Reader's Digest Writers' Award, and, in the United Kingdom, the T. S. Eliot Prize. He has received fellowships from the Guggenheim Foundation, the National Endowment for the Arts, the Ingram Merrill Foundation, and the Center for Scholars and Writers at the New York Public Library. He is a professor at the University of Houston, and he lives in New York City and in Provincetown.

SCHOOL OF THE ARTS

◆ ◆

SCHOOL OF THE ARTS

◆ ◆

POEMS

MARK DOTY

HARPER ◐ PERENNIAL

NEW YORK ● LONDON ● TORONTO ● SYDNEY

HARPER ⬤ PERENNIAL

A hardcover edition of this book was published in 2005 by HarperCollins
Publishers.

SCHOOL OF THE ARTS. Copyright © 2005 by Mark Doty. All rights
reserved. Printed in the United States of America. No part of this book may
be used or reproduced in any manner whatsoever without written permission
except in the case of brief quotations embodied in critical articles and reviews.
For information address HarperCollins Publishers, 10 East 53rd Street,
New York, NY 10022.

HarperCollins books may be purchased for educational, business, or sales
promotional use. For information please write: Special Markets Department,
HarperCollins Publishers, 10 East 53rd Street, New York, NY 10022.

FIRST HARPER PERENNIAL EDITION PUBLISHED 2006.

Designed by Lundquist Design, New York

The Library of Congress has catalogued the hardcover edition as follows:

Doty, Mark.
    School of the arts: poems / Mark Doty.—1st ed.
        p. cm.
    ISBN 0-06-075245-9
      I. Title.

PS3554.O798S34 2005
811'.54—dc22   2004047540

ISBN-10: 0-06-075246-7 (pbk.)
ISBN-13: 978-0-06-075246-0 (pbk.)

    07 08 09 10 ❖/HC 10 9 8 7 6 5 4 3 2

ACKNOWLEDGMENTS

Some of these poems have been published previously, often in earlier versions:

Bark:	"Heaven for Arden"; "Heaven for Beau"
Bloom:	"The Hood"
Columbia:	"The Bootblack"
Electronic Poetry Review:	"Signal"
Green Mountains Review:	"Meditation: 'The Night of Time'"; "The Pink Poppy"
London Review of Books:	"Heaven for Helen"; "Heaven for Paul"; "The Hours"; "Notebook / To Lucian Freud / On the Veil"
Lyric:	"Now You're an Animal"; "Time and the Town"; "To García Lorca"
Magma:	"To Caravaggio"
New Yorker:	"In the Same Space"
Ninth Letter:	"Flit"

Poetry London:	"In Their Flight"
Rattapalax:	"Shahid's Couplet"
Rattle:	"Letter to God"
Shenandoah:	"Fire to Fire"; "Late Flight"
Slate:	"Ultrasound"
The Threepenny Review:	"The Stairs"
Virginia Quarterly Review:	"School of the Arts"

"Flit" was commissioned by the Calouste Gulbenkian Foundation as part of *Wild Reckoning: An Anthology Provoked by Rachel Carson's Silent Spring* (2004).

"The Hours" was commissioned by the Research Institute at the John Paul Getty Museum in Los Angeles.

"To García Lorca" was commissioned by Poetry International, London, 2002, as a response to *Poet in New York*.

"Fire to Fire" appeared in *Best American Spiritual Writing 2004*.

Some of these poems appeared in *Fire to Fire*, a limited edition letter press volume published by Sutton Hoo Press.

I am grateful to the Lila Wallace–Reader's Digest Fund, and to the Dorothy and Lewis B. Cullman Center for Scholars and Writers at the New York Public Library, for assistance that made the writing of these poems possible.

To God—

If you have formed a Circle to go into
Go into it yourself & see how you would do

—William Blake

CONTENTS

SCHOOL OF THE ARTS

◆ ◆

Heaven for Helen

Helen says heaven, for her,
would be complete immersion
in physical process,
without self-consciousness —

to be the respiration of the grass,
or ionized agitation
just above the break of a wave,
traffic in a sunflower's thousand golden rooms.

Images of exchange,
and of untrammeled nature.
But if we're to become part of it all,
won't our paradise also involve

participation in being, say,
diesel fuel, the impatience of trucks
on August pavement,
weird glow of service areas

along the interstate at night?
We'll be shiny pink egg cartons,
and the thick treads of burst tires
along the highways in Pennsylvania:

a hell we've made to accompany
the given: we will join
our tiresome productions,
things that want to be useless forever.

But that's me talking. Helen
would take the greatest pleasure
in being a scrap of paper,
if that's what there were to experience.

Perhaps that's why she's a painter,
finally: to practice disappearing
into her scrupulous attention,
an exacting rehearsal for the larger

world of things it won't be easy to love.
Helen I think will master it, though I may not.
She has practiced a long time learning to see.
I have devoted myself to affirmation,

when I should have kept my eyes on the ground.

Flit

           —dart—an idea
arcs the cold, then a clutch

of related thoughts;
slim branches don't even

flicker with the weight
of what's landed;

animate alphabet
whizzing past our faces,

a black and white hurry,
as if a form of notation

accompanied our walk,
a little ahead of us

and a bit behind. If we
could *see* their trajectory,

if their trace remained
in the winter air,

what a tunnel they'd figure:
skein of quick vectors

above our heads,
a fierce braid,

improvised, their decisions
—the way one makes poetry

from syntax—unpredictable, resolving
to wild regularity

(thought has to flit
to describe it, speech

has to try that hurry).
A scaffolding,

a kind of argument
about being numerous.

Thread and rethread—alight.
Study. We might be carrying

crumbs. We're not. I wish.
Their small heads cock,

they lift (no visible effort,
as if flight were the work

of the will only), light,
a bit further along,

and though they're silent
it seems you could hear

the minute repeating registers
of their attention,

*_____, *_____, the *here you are*
yes here you yes.

Pronoun reference unclear.
Who looks at us

—an aerial association
of a dozen subjectivities,

or a singular self
wearing, this snowy afternoon,

twelve pair of wings?
Collectivity of sparks,

sparking collectivity? Say *live*
resides not inside feathers or skin

but in the whizzing medium.
No third person.

Sharp, clear globe of January,
and we—the fourteen of us—

the thinking taking place.
We is instances of alertness,

grammar help me.
Mind in the ringing day,

a little of us ahead
and a bit behind,

and all that action
barely disturbs the air.

Heaven for Stanley

For his birthday, I gave Stanley a hyacinth bean,
an annual, so he wouldn't have to wait for the flowers.

He said, *Mark, I have just the place for it!*
as if he'd spent ninety-eight years

anticipating the arrival of this particular vine.

I thought poetry a brace against time,
the hours held up for study in a voice's cool saline,

but his allegiance is not to permanent forms.
His garden's all furious change,

budding and rot and then the coming up again;

why prefer any single part of the round?
I don't know that he'd change a word of it;

I think he could be forever pleased
to participate in motion. Something opens.

He writes it down. Heaven steadies
and concentrates near the lavender. He's already there.

Ultrasound

Blackboard covered with a dust
    of living chalk, live chaos-cloud
        wormed by turbulence: the rod glides

and the vet narrates shadows
    I can't quite force into shape:
        His kidneys might . . . the spleen appears . . .

I can't see what he sees, and so
    resort to simile: cloudbank, galaxy
        blurred with slow comings

and goings, that far away. The doctor
    makes appreciative noises,
        to encourage me;

he praises Beau's stillness.
    I stroke the slope beneath
        those open, abstracted eyes,

patient, willing to endure whatever
    we deem necessary, while the vet
        runs along the shaved blonde

—blue-veined, gleaming with gelled alcohol
    to allow sound to penetrate
        more precisely—a kind of wand,

pointing a stream of waves
    —nothing we could hear—
        to translate the dark inside his ribs

onto this midnight screen.
    The magic pen slides, the unseen's made—
        well, far from plain.

No chartable harmony,
    less anatomy than a storm
        of pinpoints subtler than stars.

Where does a bark upspool
    from the quick,
        a baritone swell

past the sounding chambers?
    You can't see that, or the clock
        built into the wellspring,

or that fixed place from which
    a long regarding of us
        rises. It wasn't cancer,

wasn't clear, we didn't see, really,
    anything. He's having trouble
        keeping up his weight;

his old appetites flag,
    though on the damp morning trails
        he's the same golden hurry.

Today I'm herding the two old dogs
    into the back of the car,
        after the early walk, wet woods:

Beau's generous attention must be
    brought into focus, gaze pointed
        to the tailgate so he'll be ready to leap,

and Arden, arthritic in his hind legs,
    needs me to lift first his forepaws
        and then, placing my hands

under his haunches, hoist the moist
    black bulk of him into the wagon,
        and he growls a little

before he turns to face me,
    glad to have been lifted—
        And as I go to praise them,

as I like to do, the words
    that come from my mouth,
        from nowhere, are *Time's children*,

as though that were the dearest thing
    a person could say.
        Why did I call them by that name?

They race this quick parabola
    faster than we do, as though
        it were a run in the best of woods,

run in their dreams, paws twitching
    —even asleep they're hurrying.
        Doesn't the world go fast enough?

We're caught in this morning's
    last-of-April rain, the three of us
        bound and fired by duration

—rhythm too swift for even them
    to hear, though perhaps we catch
        a little of that rush and ardor

—furious poetry!—
    the sound time makes,
        seeing us through.

The Hours

Big blocks of ice
—clear cornerstones—
chug down a turning belt
toward the blades of a wicked,

spinning fan; scraping din
of a thousand skates and then
powder flies out in a roaring
firehose spray of diamond dust,

and the film crew obscures
the well-used Manhattan snow
with a replica of snow.

————

Trailers along the edge of the Square,
arc lamps, the tangled cables
of a technical art, and our park's

a version of itself. We walk here
daily, the old dogs and I glad
for the open rectangle of air

held in its frame of towers,
their heads held still and high
to catch the dog run's rich,

acidic atmosphere, whitened faces
—theirs and mine—lifted toward gray
branches veining the variable sky.

Today we're stopped at the rim:
one guy's assigned the task
of protecting the pristine field

a woman will traverse
—after countless details are worried
into place—at a careful angle,

headed toward West Fourth.
They're filming *The Hours*,
Michael's novel, a sort of refraction

of *Mrs. Dalloway*. Both books
transpire on a single June day;
that's the verb; these books do

breathe an air all attention,
as if their substance were a gaze
entirely open to experience, eager

to know—They believe
the deepest pleasure is seeing
and saying how we see,

even when we're floored
by spring's sharp grief, or a steady
approaching wave of darkness.

In the movie version, it's winter;
they're aiming for a holiday release,
and so must hasten onward.

Someone calls out *Background!*
and hired New Yorkers begin
to pass behind the perfect field,

a bit self-conscious, skaters
and shoppers too slow to convince,
so they try it again, Clarissa passing

the sandblasted arch
bound in its ring of chain-link,
monument glowing gray against the gray.

———

A little less now in the world to love.

Taxi on Bleecker, dim afternoon, after
a bright one's passing, after the hours
in stations and trains, blur of the meadows

through dull windows, fitful sleep,
heading home, and now the darkness inside
the cab deeper than anything a winter afternoon

could tender. Nothing stays, the self
has no power over time, we're stuck
in a clot of traffic, then this: a florist shop,

where something else stood yesterday,
what was it? Do things give way that fast?
PARADISE FLOWERS, arced in gold

on the window glass, racks and rows
of blooms, and an odd openness on the sidewalk,
and—look, the telltale script of cables

inking the street, trailers near, and Martian lamps,
and a lone figure in a khaki coat poised
with a clutch of blooms while they check her aspect

through the lens: Clarissa, of course,
buying the flowers herself.
I take it personally. As if,

no matter what, this emblem persists:
a woman went to buy flowers, years ago,
in a novel, and was entered

by the world. Then in another novel,
her double chose blooms of her own
while the blessed indifferent life

of the street pierced her, and now
here she is, blazing in a dim trench
of February, the present an image

reduced through a lens, a smaller version
of a room in which love resided.
Though they continue, shadow and replica,

copy and replay, adapted, reduced,
reframed: beautiful versions—a paper cone of asters,
golden dog nipping at a glove—fleeting,

and no more false than they are true.

Then the gold was gone from the world
—no, there was gold everywhere,
my gold wasn't

Notebook/To Lucian Freud/On the Veil

I love starting things

———

Fat and shadow, oil and wax,
mobility solidified,
like cooled grease in a can—

———

Seeing how far I can go

———

Analiese said, happily, "He paints the ugliness of flesh,"
    but that isn't it: flesh without the overlayer, how we ought to
see it, all we're taught—
    January sky over Seventh. To the north,
    a slab of paraffin. A wax table. Then it pinks,

shifts, at the most complicated hour, after sunset, before dark,
the lamps already on.
     A deepening blue at the sky's center, but the tops of the buildings
still warmed by the last of sunlight,
     the way he fixes the face at its most subtle hour

————

One of the things that makes you continue is the difficulty surely

————

     all the decisions of color revealed, light making available every
nuance of a (sur)face so plainly itself it's become plea and testament.

     Ugly: resist the term, or open it: the living edge resisting?
     Surface the heart of the matter.
     Strange achievement: to see skin
     as no one else.

————

Never any beauty

greater than the body hung in the ceaseless wind of time
and repeating in that current its stream of postures,

skin perpetually lit from within
as if by its own failure—

―――――

When I paint clothes I am really painting naked people who are covered in clothes

―――――

January in grisaille.
    Sarah and Lucy erased,
        weirdly euphonious terms:

lymphoma, heroin.
    Then an anonymous body
        on the sidewalk,

a fifth-floor room onto Sixth Avenue,
    the aching window open all afternoon.
        A man on our block

pulled from his car and beaten
    with a tire iron by another driver
        who wanted him to hurry up

and pass the garbage truck.
    Flesh fails and failure
        is visited upon it.

The book of Freud's paintings
        a brooding invitation, catalogue
                of human suspension in time

and today I think they're an oil
        and pigment howl,
                outpouring against limit.

But as soon as I've said it,
        the old argument resumes,
                the ambiguity of *vanitas*:

do these paintings of dying things
        warn or celebrate,

does their maker caution or consume?

My life in the fields of this argument,
shifting skin
        the live veil,

                elongated grammar of muscle,

this moment's agreement of light

on the pure actual. (No such thing as *the* body.)

Fact of a wrist.

Vein troubling a forehead.

Melville: *How can the prisoner reach outside except by thrusting through the wall?*

———

(By the water fountain in the gym)

On the huge man's left arm TRUST
above an image he called the god of joy
on his right forearm
inscribed above the veins
a centaur

symbol of leadership he said
of direction

I couldn't speak, in some deep basement of myself thinking
Maybe his great body is the fact

I require . . .

the dream of being *realized*

And half the night I'm thinking
of the immense human wall
and veil of him. What is it
we want from a body;

the lying-awake longing,
to what does it attend? Whitman:
these thoughts in the darkness why are they?

———

Clothing veils
the real;
      flesh conceals—

what to call it?
quick lively presence quickening
through the lidded eyes,

a moment's sharp attention,

the painting looking back at us?

———

The mystery isn't mind
    (what else are we, evidently,
        besides *aware?*)

but materiality, intersection
    of solidity and flame,
        where quick and stillness meet—

Materiality the impenetrable thing.
    We don't know what it *is*
        other than untrustworthy—

all bodies, even the young,
    who rightly think
        they're untouchable:

that faith's their signature
    and credential.
        I am a body less reliable,

and therefore the rough-scumbled peaks
    of these faces thrill, familiar—
        aspects of flesh breaking here,

the way we say waves *break*—
    become visible at the instant
        of their descent.

Caught somewhere in the arc.
    How will these look
        in a hundred years?

Stunningly *here*.

———

Intricate wall
of appearances—

lit at its highest entablatures,

water towers and rooftops, cornice and capital,
    smokestack and chimneypot picked out

by the glow slanting across the river,
    intensified Hudson-light,

and warm lamps in the high windows,
    neon over the shopfronts

flickering on:

world of consummate detail.

The city lay back,
shambling, corpulent, nude
        (why he loves the big frame:

because it is no longer
        flesh
    but *the* flesh)

———

Nothing ever stands in for anything. Nobody is representing anything.

———

My god: every body
of a piece, every factual expanse of skin,
the contour of them—

that's what language can't do, curve and heft of it,
that stretch . . . Oil and shadow,
fat and wax, grief solidified.

There's no one else.
You and I the common apprehension of this.

———

Our chests open, arms back,
the teacher said, "This is a position
of FIERCE VULNERABILITY—"

I thought, That's it, that's
exactly a position one could live
toward, to stand in permeable faith,

and yet such force in that stance,
upright, heart thrust out
to the world, unguarded, no hope

without the possibility of a wound.
"To hold oneself in this pose," he said,
"takes incredible strength."

_____

Everything is autobiographical

_____

I look at his pictures and want
above all language muscling up,
active work of pushing out some sound,
throat and muscle of the tongue,

some hope of accuracy—

_____

and everything is a portrait, even if it's a chair

_____

Accuracy? Go on, then—

to write the tragedy of this body

_____

I want to go on until there is nothing more to see

In the Same Space

The sun set early in the Square, winter afternoons,
angling over the apartments to the west, so that light would bisect

the northern row of dark houses diagonally, the grand houses
that were suddenly not of the last century but of the century
    before.

Then the world would seem equally divided, awhile, between
    the golden
and the chill, equipoise in a bitter year. When the sun was
    completely gone,

we'd turn for home, the dogs and I, and to the south, the two
    towers,
harshly formal by day, brusque in their authority—

at the beginning of evening they'd go a blue a little darker than
    the sky,
lit from top to bottom by a wavering curtain of small, welcoming
    lamps.

Shahid's Couplet

Your old kitchen, dear, on Bleecker: sugar, dates, black tea.
Your house, then ours. Anyone's now. Memory's furious land.

Oncoming Train

I hate that moment when the train's coming
into the station, hurtling, inviting, so ferocious in its forward momentum,

the most dangerous thirty seconds of my day, twice every day,
sometimes more; sometimes I have to steady myself against a pillar

on the platform, or stand at a distance, against the back wall,
in order to feel that I will more firmly resist the impulse.

Not that I want to be dead, exactly, and certainly not
that I want to suffer, I have a great deal to live for—

But the idea of simply stepping out of forwardness
—that moment is the clearest invitation and opportunity

to strike against time, to refuse to accede, to win some power
over what no one controls. I'm not proud of this,

I wouldn't tell just anyone, but I will tell you.
The train's a huge onrushing refusal,

and who has any power over time, save to refuse?

Or no:
to hurry time, to *make him run*—that is a radical form of submission.

Heaven for Paul

The flight attendant said,
We have a mechanical problem with the plane,
and we have contacted the FAA for advice,

and then, *We will be making an emergency landing in Detroit,*

and then, *We will be landing at an air force base in Dayton,*
because there is a long runway there, and because
there will be a lot of help on the ground.

Her voice broke slightly on the word *help*,
and she switched off the microphone, hung it back on its hook,
turned to face those of us seated near her,
and began to weep.

Could the message have been more clear?
Around us people began to cry themselves,
or to pray quietly, or to speak to those with whom
they were traveling, saying the things that people
would choose to say to one another before
an impending accident of uncertain proportion.

It was impossible to hear, really, the details
of their conversations—it would have been wrong to try—
but one understood the import of the tones of voice
everywhere around us, and we turned to each other,

as if there should have been some profound things to be imparted,
but what was to be said seemed so obvious and clear:
that we'd had a fine few years, that we were terrified
for the fate of our own bodies and each other's,
and didn't want to suffer, and could not imagine

the half-hour ahead of us. We were crying a little
and holding each other's hands, on the armrest;
I was vaguely aware of a woman behind us, on the aisle,
who was startled at the sight of two men holding hands,

and I wondered how it could matter to her, now,
on the verge of this life—and then I wondered how it could
    matter to me,
that she was startled, when I flared on that same margin.

The flight attendant instructed us in how to brace
for a crash landing—to remove our glasses and shoes
and put our heads down, as we did long ago, in school,
in the old days of civil defense. We sat together, quietly.
And this is what amazed me: Paul,

who of the two of us is the more nervous,
the less steadily grounded in his own body,
became completely calm. Later he told me

how he visualized his own spirit
stepping from the flames, and visited,
in his picturing, each person he loved,
and made his contact and peace with each one,

and then imagined himself turning toward
what came next, an unseeable *ahead*.
                                        For me,
it wasn't like that at all. I had no internal composure,

and any ideas I'd ever entertained about dying
seemed merely that, speculations flown now
while my mind spiraled in a hopeless sorrowful motion,

sure I'd merely be that undulant fuel haze
in the air over the runway, hot chemical exhaust,
atomized, no idea what had happened to me,

what to do next, and how much of the next life
would I spend (as I have how much of this one?)
hanging around an airport. I thought of my dog,

and who'd care for him. No heaven for me,
only the unimaginable shape of not-myself—
and in the chaos of that expectation,

without compassion, unwilling,
I couldn't think beyond my own dissolution.
What was the world without me to see it?

And while Paul grew increasingly radiant,

the flight attendant told us it was time to crouch
into the positions we had rehearsed,
the plane began to descend, wobbling,

and the tires screeched against the runway,
burning down all but a few feet of five miles of asphalt
before it rolled its way to a halt.

We looked around us, we let go
the long held breath, the sighs and exhalations,
Paul exhausted from the effort of transcendence,

myself too pleased to be breathing to be vexed
with my own failure, and we were still sitting and beginning to laugh
when the doors of the plane burst open,

and large uniformed firemen came rushing down the aisles,
shouting *Everybody off the plane, now, bring nothing with you,*
leave the plane immediately

—because, as we'd learn in the basement
of the hangar where they'd brought us,
a line of tornadoes was scouring western Ohio,
approaching the runway we'd fled.

At this point it seemed plain: if God intervenes
in history, it's either to torment us
or to make us laugh, or both, which is how

we faced the imminence of our deaths the second time.
I didn't think once about my soul, as we waited in line,
filing into the hangar, down into the shelter

—where, after a long while, the National Guard would bring us
boxes and boxes of pizza, and much later, transport us, in buses,
to complimentary hotel rooms in Cincinnati.

To García Lorca

A whole acre's containment and release,
yellow exhalation; stiff stalk and copper blaze
blaring into the Seventh Avenue A.M.
      —sunflowers,

in a square rusting tub casually set
on the linoleum of the corner market
on 17th Street, where the large brusque
      and tender Rumanian

barks your order back at you, then places
change in your hand like a benediction.
Against the wall, away from the counter,
      sulphurous heads

fused into one radiating distillate
of the infinitive *to bloom*.
And almost entirely ignored, since
      we understand,

even in the eight-o'clock scurry toward
purpose commerce engagement,
that the principal beauty of New York lies
        in human faces.

But these foot soldiers of summer—flown
from a Mexican field, boxed north
from Alabama?—neck to neck in an impossible crowd,
        they're our double

and mirror: a hundred fierce dawns
up to their hard green waists
in cool water, shocking
        in their sameness

and startling again in the shag
variations of their faces dreaming . . .
nothing language knows. Though they
        are dreaming,

gazes both open and elsewhere
at once. And in this way also resemble us,
half asleep still, unworldly, carrying our sacks
        of coffee prepared

as we have requested it, this town's
flowering and respiration conducted
through our ten thousand acres'
        bud and scatter.

This morning on 16th a dragonfly
—intricate, upside down, probably lost but entirely
self-possessed—clung to a brownstone wall,
        immobile,

a cistern's discolored bronze. Fountain
of refreshment, still point of the neighborhood
while taxis fret the air wild between the curbs,
        already honking

and braking the song of ongoing and indifferent
setting out, same chorus as my tub of bloom:
basket refilling itself to fuel the multitude
        who doesn't want them,

since we are already flowers, already carry
shoulder to shoulder that diffident power,
stand even now stalk to stripped stalk
        in the killing tub,

enough water to sustain a little while,
flaring out at the pores, out through
this dark-rimmed,
        gold-dusted seeing.

In Their Flight

Who believes in them?

It doesn't matter much
to the souls, newly set free,
wheeling in the air over the site

of their last engagements.
Suppose we could see them?
They'd be like sparrows—no *like,*

they'd *be* birds, one of those autumn flocks

when the solitaries gather in great numbers
over the waste places and the remaining fields,
turning in the air as if together they made a huge piece of cloth

folding in on itself, or a mathematical diagram of folding . . .
No hurry, nothing obscuring the air for them—
vast sky, entirely light-washed,

as they assemble into a great progression of pattern.
In community at last, we want to proceed in our flock, our troop . . .

———

Incorporated into a radiant vitality without ceasing . . .

You want more than that?

Of course you do: you want the steady
mosquito-drone to go on and on, ceaselessly,

you want to be the one who gets to do the perceiving
forever, of course you do.

———

But here's my guess:

it's another thing for the dead;
they've been singular long enough.
We can't let ourselves see what
enormous work it is
to be one of something, to exert
the will to sustain those boundaries.
The dead, rimless,

loosed from particularity,
move out toward the edge of the city,
someplace the flock can unknot itself

freely, where they can feast in the fields
oblivious to the column of smoke roiling behind them.

———

Anniversary day, evil wind banging the door to the gym
till the glass shattered, and Mauricio said,
—in a low voice, as if to say it would somehow protect him—

Lot of spirits blowing around today

Letter to God

The dogs were tired and bewildered,
stunned by the ways they'd been treated
by men—yelled at, kicked around, left unfed
in the cold and the rain. Not to mention

the usual predations: cold creak
of the hips, tumor and clouded eye,
ears that ceased to help at all . . .
What could they do,

to whom might they appeal?
The wisest among them
—that was his reputation—
suggested that a letter be drafted to God;

only by appeal to a higher authority
might their plight be considered.
But once the questions were written,
who would carry it? Who knew how

to imagine the way?
The ablest was chosen—a retriever,
nearly incapable of flagging,
and his entire being knew the imperative

to carry. But how will you carry it?
they asked. In my mouth. No, they cried,
you'll drop it every time you bark.
And then the wisest made this plan:

they'd roll their plea into a scroll,
tightly, and their hero would open
his legs, and lift his tail, and carry
the missive inside him,

where he was sure to keep it
until he reached the gates of paradise.
And off he trotted, head high, and tail,
only a slight delicacy in his walk

betraying discomfort, into the fields
with their blonde grasses, upstream,
off toward the border of the world.
Do I need to tell you he never returned?

Why, Lord, the letter read, *did you put
a wicked clockspring in our bellies?
Our eyes glaze, our old hips refuse
a step, we can't even lift a leg*

to mark a trail. Why given these indignities
are we further subject to the harrowing
of men, we who stand before them
all expectation, why are we met with blows,

or worse? In every town of this world
you've given us, in pen and shelter,
in cellar and alley and hole in the dirt,
we your children await your reply.

Therefore, when each dog meets a stranger,
it's necessary to sniff beneath the tail:
perhaps, this time, this is the returning messenger;
it's still possible a reply might reach them.

Signal

LOST COCKATIEL, cried the sign, hand-lettered,
taped to the side of a building: *last seen on 16th*

between Fifth and Sixth, gray body, orange cheek patches,
yellow head. Name: Omar. Somebody's dear, I guess,

though how do you lose a cockatiel on 16th Street?
Flown from a ledge, into the sky he's eyed

for months or years, into the high limbs of the ginkgos,
suddenly free? I'm looking everywhere in the rustling

globes and spires shot through with yellow,
streaking at the edges, for any tropic flash of him. Why

should I think I'd see him, in the vast flap this city is?
Why wander Chelsea when that boy could be up and gone,

winging his way to Babylon or Oyster Bay,
drawn to some magnet of green. Sense to go south?

Not likely; Omar's known the apartment and the cage,
picked his seeds from a cup, his fruits and nuts from the hand

that anchored him—and now, he's launched, unfindable,
no one's baby anymore but one bit . . .

Think of the great banks of wires and switches
in the telephone exchange, every voice and signal

a little flicker lighting up—that's Omar now,
impulse in the propulsive flow. Who'll ever know?

Then this morning we're all in the private commuter blur
when a guy walks into the subway car whistling,

doing birdcalls; he's decked in orange and lime,
a flag pluming his baseball cap; he's holding out a paper cup

while he shifts from trills to caws. Not much of a talent,
I think, though I like his shameless attempt at charm,

and everybody's smiling covertly, not particularly tempted
to give him money. Though one man reaches into his pocket

and starts to drop some change into the cup,
and our Papageno says, "That's my coffee, man,

but thanks, God bless you anyway,"
and lurches whistling out the door.

Now You're an Animal

I'd expected to sit for my portrait
in the photographer's studio—
chilly morning, fierce April wind on Sixth
slicing through my jacket and sweater,

new blur of the trees overhead—
but at the loft, a huge roll of white paper
hung from the ceiling, blocking a wall of windows;

he handed me a bucket of black paint
and brushes and said, Now, how would you
like to represent yourself? I wasn't ready
for that. It wasn't noon, I'd hurried across

the city, and didn't feel awake to the task
of metaphor. Then we were talking, easy, about
what others had done—he photographed painters,

actors, whoever he liked in the arts—
and how dancers often leapt before the white field
he'd offered them. And I said,
I've always wanted antlers, and began to paint

high on the big page black reindeer horns,
in thick strokes, the paint dripping nicely,
and when I finished I could stand

beneath them and the serious, branching
architecture seemed to spring from my head.
He stood at the other end of the room,
framing me upside down in his lens. He said,

That's wonderful, what do you want to wear?
I didn't know. He said, Take off your shirt,
and I did, and he said, Now you're an animal!

I ripped open the buttons of my jeans
so as to be a lustful beast, and he cried,
Yes, that's it! And though it was a joke
still I was seized by a sort of heat;

I took deep breaths, tilted my head up,
stood in the center of my own authority
while he lifted sheets of film and pushed

others in again, and clicked the lens.
He said, That's good, what else? I don't know
how else to do it unless you're naked.
And I said, I'm okay with that, and without

even my watch or ring, only the arching
crown tangling high into the air above me,
I felt the up-pushing pulse of some originating flame.

I thought, This is the relation between narrative
and lyric: one minute you're on 23rd Street
trying to find an address, and the next
you're naked under a wet crown of horns.

That's how fast we slip into the underlife.
Later, out in the daylight, I thought,
What if my students see this picture?

or the Dean of Liberal Arts?—but only
after I'd walked back out into
the elevator and the lobby, onto the sidewalk
with an odd warmth banked inside me,

creaturely: the undertime, beneath
the new haze of trees overhead,
bud time, the sharp spring wind

equal parts ice and green. What is lyric?
I wanted the animal seen
that I might know him. Even
waiting at the blustery intersections,

I was warmed by the incipient leaves,
and I held the antlers high in the wind,
their heat radiating down into my face,

and on the street a few men knew what I wished:
that my plain clothes hid hooves and haunches.

The Vault

And Craving said,
. . . Why do you lie, since you belong to me?

The Gospel of Mary Magdalene

1. The Bootblack

What can be said of this happiness?
The bootblack boy on his knees
in the dim of the bar gives himself
completely to the work of polishing,

leaning into the body on the stool
before him, a shirtless and eager man
who's being mouthed clean.
Around them parts the human dark.

Not much to do with degradation;
the generous bootblack pours
his attention out of his body
—all alertness—into the presence

before him, up the legs, beautiful,
burying his face in the warm cloth
of the lap: completed, receptacle,
recipient, held, filled—

Though it's hardly passive:
he's working to relinquish,
giving the seated one pleasure,
releasing his own weight.

They seem to light the gloom
of their corner; together
they make one lamp. And as if
his work were not complete

until it had been seen by another
—labor of the mouth,
art perfected with the tongue—
he turns his face up toward me,

his witness, smiling, though the verb's
thin for this unshielded triumph
of a face: What's he conquered?
Distance and dissatisfaction have slipped

from the look he lifts to me,
so that his power might not go
unacknowledged, now that
he is the image of achieved joy.

2. Double Embrace

Skin to the back of me,
skin to the fore,

and I'm the center
of a double embrace,

or perhaps that's not
the precise term,

since no one's
face to face; we are

three shirtless men
become one

tentative whole,
the thick arms behind me

pressing against my arms,
then reaching forward

to the arms before me,
drawing us tighter together,

heat and slow
uprush of it; no hurry,

the embrace rocking
a bit, a bit of motion

to bind three disparate
bodies into—Look what we can make!

Six arms snaking,
so that the darkened barroom

recedes, and the mirrors,
the pendant lanterns and bluish

video haze. Then the firm hands
kneading my shoulders, hands

over my heart, my hands
on the shoulders in front of me,

those arms reached back toward
the original arms, as though

we were the chain of generation,
each man proceeding from the one

before, and each also reaching
backward, into the body

which had borne him—
The bar's a cave of minor

miracle played out—
it's not sex I want, if what sex *is*

is coming; more than that,
search and pleasure, reading,

divining signals, shift of attention,
flare in my direction, pose,

tattooed arms gleaming, hips
cocked in their particular invitation.

Particular! We're almost generalized
here, local avatars

of a broader principle,
we are just now representative men

doing the men's work
—fierce vulnerability—

open and containing, open
and held, the forward momentum

ceased, swaying a little, a few minutes,
before the triangle breaks apart.

belly hard in the small of my back,
kiss to the back of my neck,

and I lean forward to kiss
the neck before me.

3. To Caravaggio

The Hispanic boy beside me—nude, only mildly muscled,
a slight tracing of hair above the heart-searing curve of his upper lip—
is next in line for a massage, so he lies down on the pool table,

covered tonight with a sheet of black plywood, a black tarp,
and long rows of paper towels. He's so finely white he's nearly blue,
and as the masseur begins—first a light coating of oil for traction,

then the rub in earnest; down the back, working the neck
and shoulders, the long thighs, turning him over, polishing
the long abdomen, raising toward the ceiling lamp

the firm and slender chest. And now he seems a cadaver,
laid out, or a boy posing as a corpse, inert, eyes at ease,
mouth entirely tranquil. All in a ring around the table,

young men and grizzled elders watching,
and two splendid witnesses like visiting kings
without their fine robes, their perfect skin shading into the darkness.

Then the masseur lifts the arms above the head, to stretch
the lats and shoulders, and suddenly the boy's the corpus of our Lord
still nailed to his cross, shockingly real, the dark of the room

composing itself, in lustrous blacks, around the suspended body.

4. Hood

A master leads his slave
    through the bar,

the slighter man bound
    to his lodestar

by a leash hooked
    to his collar,

every surface of him swathed,
    rubber, leather,

hard to tell in this light.
    Slits in the hood,

almost nothing of him
    visible. They look,

I think, ridiculous
    —but something

compelling about it, too:
    only an outside:

absurd, elaborate universe
    of buckles and straps,

every bit of the body
    sealed away,

so nothing of the interior
    can be known.

From a distance sex looks,
    inevitably, awful:

what's less graceful
    than transport?

Face focused
    to a single point,

clenched, contorted, or the mouth
    stretched wide—

Therefore this exterior's sealed,
    blank, so that we might

guess at what lies
    beneath: happy abdication,

the will locked down at last,
    unable to choose

or to act. Who knows?
    Impenetrable,

what's paraded before us.

5. The Acknowledgment

Waves breaking in darkness,
a crowd of shadows,
severe hand on my back,

pushing me down,
that's what you want,
to be held down, to be forced,

of course it sounds ugly,
but that's the difference
between the interior

and the limit of saying;
the mouth won't make
what the spirit knows,

so say it roughly
or not at all: to be made
to receive, which I did,

gladly. My pleasure.
And the towering man
bent down and took my face

in his big hand,
looked directly into my eyes
and said, "Thank you,"

as if I had honored him,
in some fashion,
through my submission.

And in truth that was what
I liked best, the being acknowledged
—that was the difficult thing.

6. The Harness

Pliny saw a centaur,
brought from Egypt,
pickled in brine and honey

—salt and sweetness,
strange preservatives—
emblem hung there

in his dreaming
—hot musk of the flanks,
thick hooves, the glass vault

large enough, almost,
for a man half-equine
caught in his embalmed sleep,

permanent, in suspension.

7. The Blessing

They were deep in the mine of souls
—no, I mean they'd gone far
into that shaft where inner and outer

grow indissoluble, dark against dark,
say beneath a bridge at night, where long attention
allows a sense of the breathing rippling;

they were practicing, heavy boots
above them, moving a little, above the grid
of a floor like those of stacked prison cells

—a brig, a Piranesian chamber, a cavern of men—

they were immersed in the night
when something warm—at first they knew not
what, they had no understanding, in the darkness—

another—sudden droplet—*small rain*—
Reader, I have no adequate term
for what blessed them, no word commensurate.

Then he conceived what he could:
a notion: if he remained in his body

(constrained within
the bond of a perimeter
simultaneously fixed and permeable,

if he were stayed, if he held fast—)

then he would break into flower.

Late Flight

The pilot of the little plane must stop his engines
while fifty pounds of sand are lugged into the nose
to balance out our weight. He explains, turns his key

in the ignition—sputter, whine, nothing.
Again: grind and cough, nothing. Ripple of doubt.
Third time: unpromising silence and then the motor

shudders awake, and we taxi till we face
a swath of black pavement bound by rowed lamps
—then race and lift so swiftly our collective weight

seems nothing at all. Over the dim marshland,
a bit of bay, rows of rooftops bordering the shore,
the harbor islands with their lighthouses.

And turning back to look—we all turn back to look—
—what is it these glittering fields are like?
One wants words, but words are wanting,

figures worn: deltas and archipelagoes,
red nerves, coppery rivulets of a freeway's
arcing ramps. Then further, higher: hot jewels.

Scintillant flakes on a video screen. Better:
holes in black paper, an immense page
held between us and an overwhelming realm,

so that just this clattering glare comes
bursting through, just enough that we can bear to see . . .

Which seems to prepare us, somehow,
to turn in the other direction, toward the place
we're headed—nothing now but a tonal,

seamless night, darkness made intimate.
By all the lamps we've seen, whose multiplicity
made this warm field seem serene?

Or by the panel of instruments,
plate-glass green beneath the windshield,
the churning engine that faithfully pulls us

into the huge, physical dark.
As if it were all that's unsaid,
untranslated into the busy syllables of light.

Not afraid. Home in a while. No sign
of the town yet, glowing in its crook
of peninsula, its dim nest of sea.

Lustrous, continuous, unspoken night.
The self isn't made of language;
the self is made of night.

Fire to Fire

All smolder and oxblood,
these flowerheads,
flames of August:

fierce bronze,
or murky rose,
petals concluded in gold—

And as if fire called its double down,

the paired goldfinches
come swerving quick
on the branching towers,

so the blooms
sway with the heft
of hungers

indistinguishable, now,
from the blossoms.

Tannic yellow, or rust,

a single brassy streak
at each mid-petal
colluding in a bull's-eye ring,

copper circle
around the seed-horde
flashing like a solar flare.

You can't finish looking:
they rear and wave
in pentecostal variety.

You might as well be tracing flames.

———

Maybe nothing gold
can stay separate—
not feather flower fire.
My work's to say
what signals here,
but Lord I cannot
see a single thing.

———

If I were a sunflower I would be
the branching kind,

my many faces held out
in all directions, all attention,

awake to any golden
incident descending;

drinking in the world

with my myriads of heads,
I'd be my looking.

———

Painters have painted their swarming groups and the centre-figure of all,
From the head of the centre-figure spreading a nimbus of gold-color'd light,
But I paint myriads of heads, but paint no head without its nimbus of
    gold-color'd light . . .

———

Their rattling August clothes,
faces a swirl of hours,

                              coil in the seed
unwound at last to these
shag faces bent
over the ruining garden:

Warm evening,
                    vertical
and gold,

stalk of the body,
glistening hairs
radiating out from the curled

and lifted leaves

paired along the stalk, pattern
plunging toward the center
like the line of the thighs . . .

———

Paul said when the neighbor's puppy
ran across the street, into traffic,
because it wanted to see our dogs,
it looked like "a little flame."

———

Nothing gold can stand
apart from any other; the sunflowers are trafficked

by birds, open to bees and twilight,
implicated, alert: fire longs to meet itself
flaring, longing wants
a multiplicity of faces,

branching and branching out,

heads mouths eyes
wishing always to
double their own heat.

Which is why the void can make nothing lasting:

the fuse resides in the yellow candling up, signaling,
and the concomitant yellow hurrying down to meet it,

and nothing that is fixed
can call its double down from heaven;

                                        the gold calls to the gold
in the arc and rub,
calls to itself in the other,
                              which is why
the corona'd seedhead flashes the finches down.

Meditation: "The Night of Time"

Snow circling the steeples,
one chilly boat in the bay's dull mirror,
cold morning after Christmas,

and on the way
home from town
                    —old dog
                hobbling in the wet,
little bursts of steps, a rest,
another, shorter burst, a rest—

        I'm contemplating a phrase
quoted by candlelight
            at the Meeting House:
                            We live
                in the night of time.

Oxen in the stable, the donkey,
thick nostrils steaming,
                their clear-eyed taking-in

of the god in the hay: same
                open unmediated way
                        they see everything:

gaze unclouded by duration.
        What does Arden see,
                through the scratched
oil-patches of his cataracts,
limping home
        in the snow-turning-rain,
                old hips, slow progress

up the street from the harbor?
        Isn't the great power
                of animal eyes

that we can't read them?
And therefore something
        of the dayspring about them;

all the unsayable
        a part of one continuous . . .

My dear boy,
walking further
into the realm
of the speechless.
Night of time, daylight
of the unmeasured—

then it isn't the darkness
            that's infinite, is it?
Imagine the sort of sky
flung over this town
Christmas Eve,
            just before nightfall

(all of four-thirty, these days
when the world shuts down early
            for lack of customers):

baroque evening: wild clarity
out over the harbor,
            but to the south a louring

mood above a street
            shining greenly
            in storm-light.

And in between those two poles
            —bracing, alcohol-flame blue
                  and that deepest sable—

            stretches a shifting,
flickered, most of it, a warm plum,
            brandy, had it been a flavor,

a heated flush spreading . . .
    Maybe that's the sort of night
time is—

        rippling even as you look,
            and if the whole thing races
            toward darkness

first there's this. If that's
the night of time, Mark,
what's so bad about that?

The Stairs

Back when Arden could still climb our stairs
—sharply pitched, turning near the top,
the sort old carpenters modeled on the stairways of ships—

he'd follow Paul up to his study, shadow me
up for socks or a clean shirt. Even if I went upstairs only

for a minute, he'd wheeze and labor on the narrow steps,
and arrive out of breath, proud of himself,
and collapse on the rug before coming down again.

Up and down, all day. At night, he wanted to sleep
in his bed at the foot of ours, wanted it so badly
the pressure intensified the climb,

what with the tall risers and his gimpy hind legs. So he cried,
and fussed, and tried, gave up and went away, came back

and tried again. If he couldn't make it on his own,
I'd get up and help him, lifting his front paws
and setting them into place, then my hands under his hips;

the stairwell would smell of his anxiety: bodily,
familiar, slightly acid. Once he could no longer climb

something so awkward, it was as if he'd forgotten
he ever wanted to; he'd wedge his muzzle
into a hole he'd made in the sliding screen door,

push it to the left, and sleep all night in the garden,
on the gravel beneath the spread of a Montauk daisy.

Why can't I hold on to that image: the dreamer
beneath black leaves and a spatter of summer stars?
Indelible, that old man scent,

the fear that makes the stairway steeper.

The Art Auction

As if the soul of the town were laid out,
displayed in the auditorium at Town Hall

(velvet-curtained stage, a horseshoe balcony
ringing a wide arena of drafty winter air),
here's a century hauled down from attics,

pulled from closets and neglected walls:
modernities, one after the other:

watercolored woodblocks of bohemians
who fled the Village for light and cheap rents,
their flattened tiers of piers and houses stacked

high within the frame; Cubist constructions
—more piles of blocks, after someone's winter

in France—and then biomorphic shapes
looming from some grave collectivity,
then pure paint: brushstroke and gesture

dominate big pushy sprawls, tawny fields
brushed in blacks and grays—waves

of the newest thing now quaint, historical,
and mostly dreadful—especially the last forty
years or so, whose period styles don't seem

remote enough to charm: not these psychedelic collages,
these beach-drift assemblages, or haunted faces

peering out of—a Rorschach bloodclot
meant to conjure hell? Who'll buy this stuff?
A crowd of bidders—a few we know, mostly not,

dealers in town for an afternoon, holidayers,
condo owners out to deck their new high-ceilinged

halls with some token of the local. Abstraction,
instances of pure form? *No opening bid.*

Pass it then. Location, location; why else buy
some orange-and-lavender neo-Impressionist
portrait of the bay, or a cottage splashed in roses,

an earnest fisherman earnestly sketched?
The local sells, and numbers flash more freely,

hands leaping into air. *This driftwood whale?*
I have a hundred all over the house! Still, mixed in
among the junk, evidences of actual enchantment,

craft rising to meet the painter's plain delight
in a row of varnished trees beside some Dutch canal,

or the lifted, backlit foam of a wave curling
half a canvas high, or some lean friend's
angled torso tapered to a bare twist of waist,

those low-slung sailor pants studied, rendered,
adored. If the paint has darkened or abraded,

the stretcher pushed against the linen till it's torn,
those sunny shoulders are beloved still;
these crooked houses mount in crooked tiers

their windy hill; that coldest swell will never break,
not while this town's steeples poke up into the night.

We've been here our hour, and failed to buy
the drawing that we chose; a penciled,
freewheeling heap of geometry signed

Emily Farnham, Provincetown, 1950,
her signature formal, large as the angled strokes

intended to make sound visible, as if
she sketched some wry phrase of Poulenc,
or a serious saxophone. We didn't know

her famous teacher had corrected her work,
in the upper right hand corner, sketching

his own quick version of her forms—his hand,
it's true, far firmer than hers. His mark drives
the bidding wild. Oh well; we'd wanted it an hour,

and in an hour will think of it no more.
Now someone else has bought a tiny Hans Hofmann,

scribbled onto Emily's page. We bundle up,
out the double doors, hungry and late,
but pause as who would not at the vestibule windows,

high over the postcard view, the ring of stacked houses
fronting the twilight expanse of bay beneath

a new-starred December so blue, who could say?
Art's all bad, isn't it; what doesn't fail?
And thus there's something noble about the crap, too,

the hopeful and misguided as much a part
of this town's soul as any achievement is. We live
by our intentions, after all. Orion, his vertical belt faint,

three stars bewitched by woodsmoke,
hangs horizontal in that blue so clear and deep

words must simply slink away, defeated villains
in some grade-school play—who will, of course,
return for the next performance, trying again,

before the story winds on to the comfort of their defeat,
and all's made well again, and our town can sleep,

safely indescribable, though painted again and again,
its secrets intact, only a little of it sold.

The Pink Poppy

                                   opened in the night,
just one blossom, and when you step out
into the new air it "takes your breath away,"
as beauty is said to do: suddenly

you're flaring, open
at the top of yourself as the petals are, loose,
fringed at the edges, their interior

splotched a black already fading
toward plum, fringe and flare
wavering, in the rain,

early storm
—four-part thunder . . .
That pink lip held up

while heaven turns
in on itself, rumbling—

———

But there—you aren't supposed
to talk about beauty, are you?

———

Poor Arden's hiding under my desk;
when the thunder comes he seems to constrict himself,
and then a few moments later he's breathing heavily,

deaf as he is, holding himself taut in vigilance.
The poppy's erect
and undulant in the rain;

a sort of terrestrial jellyfish,
wavering blot like a shape on an old film,
light spot in the eye after something bright,

ragged central polyp of seed
—dark nipple-colored anemone—
held up like a sexual display . . .

Blake: *Exuberance is Beauty*.

———

Grace catches you out like a hook,
you're pulled out of yourself, a moment,

and that's the ache: peculiar blow,
reminded you aren't who you think you are.

To join oneself to this breathing pink chalice—

You want more than that?

———

A fire with a darkness in the center,
rippling interstices of night and flame . . .

Incorporated in a radiant vitality:

you want more than that?

———

Dangerous, to hate the thing that brings you all of this:
that flower wouldn't blaze if time didn't burn,

my golden dog rusting now under the roof of the garden
wouldn't have been either—no flecked ruffle
of the jowl, inner lip pink and loose . . .

And Arden: old pink muzzle sniffing now at the rain.

Brief, but no one wishes it never.

———

Theories of Beauty

1. Hook that pulls us out of time

2. or a lure to catch us in it

3. Rupture in the boundary
   caused by delight, recognition of what
   we aren't, then suddenly are?

4. Longing solidified

5. Flaunts some flaw
   —evanescence, radical pink—
   and owns that quality
   so firmly it triumphs

6. Rilke: *You, you only, exist.*
   We pass away, till at last,
   our passing is so immense
   that you arise: beautiful moment,
   in all your suddenness . . .

7. The moment budded out of us?

———

Pink fist.	Iron frill.
Essential frippery.	Fierce embroidery.
Core decor.	Severe extravagance.
Lip of otherness.	Evidence.

———

It was the pink crown of hellfire
(if hell means traffic in time)

arisen out of the earth in spring;

the vernal breaking-out
of the underglow,

and you wanted to touch it,
to be instructed by those flames
—cool and tempting—

and in a while, the rain bent
the stem to the gravel.

Heaven for Beau

Because I used to have trouble
keeping my gym locks, and trouble
learning new combinations,

I began to make small poems,
mnemonics, associating a word

with a number and thus calling up
little narratives, though the only phrases
I could remember were those

whose intent I could use:
4–20–24 became *Behind the door*

there is plenty, and behind the plenty
there is more—an affirmation,
I knew, once I'd repeated it,

to do with faring well in the world.
Then I thought it had to do with time

—couldn't there be more?—
and then with love. Abundance
could to a certain degree be trusted.

I lost that one. Then 7–26–4 became
Heaven be quick to open the door,

which I thought was for myself
at first, but I wasn't in any hurry;
it was for my golden companion,

whose form had begun to admit
imperfection, who'd begun to fail,
and if it had to be that way,

quickly then, no struggle, leap—

Then I lost that one.
On one of his last walks, he stopped
on the corner of Thompson and Prince,

nostrils startlingly wide with the scent
drifted from a lunchstand soup kitchen's

open window. Believe me,
a dog's gaze opens, like ours,
when the world's an invitation;

it was a summons, the smell of that soup,
and every reason to continue in this life.

35–9–15, I tried
(*alive, fine, sheen*)
but every consolation I rang

rhymed false, until I dreamed
a deep basement beneath the house,

and all the gone dogs drifting
forward there, in the same direction, away.

And he said—I could hear
his thinking, in the dream—
I want to go with them!

What did I know? Maybe
what he wanted was nothing

I'd ever imagine. 35–9–15;
no matter what the numbers
I could say the old poem:

35 could rhyme with *heaven*,
and 9 with *quick*, and fifteen *door*,

and I say these words almost daily,
—to the *next*—
and I have never lost that lock.

Time and the Town

Mrs. Ajo planted these:
single, utterly durable, red.
Mr. Ajo used to walk up the street
from the bay with a bucket of clams

and a cigarette fixed in his mouth
as though he'd been born
with these accessories.
They're gone now.

The poppies, in June, forthright,
like a single stripe of the flag,
all along one side of their closed-up
house: insistent, unqualified color,

and a hundred furred green
buds lift, on their bowed necks,
preparing a further outcry.
When I say I hate time, Paul says

how else could we find depth
of character, or grow souls?
Of course he's right,
but I can't help thinking

the Ajos wouldn't vote
for the mottled, complexified
shades favored by the years;
they liked this intransigent red,

they wanted it plain
and dependable, noisy.
Even Mr. Ajo, who once looked
at my garden in full bloom,

all old roses and peonies,
and said, talking around his cigarette,
Lot of money in that.

School of the Arts

The spring the Methodist Church
lost its steeple—no pointy tip
but a kind of cupola, octagonal,
with eight unglazed arches,
and on its top a carved scroll finial

signaling the tip of the builders'
skyways ambitions—a huge crane
plucked the tower like an ornament
from a cake, and lowered it to the grass
lightly. A minor revelation,

after looking up at it all these years;
who expects to get that close
to what points to heaven? Now
we could study the salt-peeled paint
along the spindled balustrades,

and peer inside, and see—who knew?—
the bell, not heard to ring
since the Methodists decamped,
their severe white ark become
a museum instead. Two, actually:

first a temple of the arts, and then,
when the wealthy patron blew town
taking his de Koonings with him,
a historical museum, locally run,
reliably dusty. I liked especially

a sentimental poet's cluttered
dune-shack study, re-created
in diorama, down to his sandals
and heaped, discarded drafts.
Up in the building's highest reaches

—huge thing, how many Methodists
could they reasonably have expected?—
the Historical Society placed its prize,
a replica of the *Rose Dorothea*,
a schooner that brought this town fame,

in the old century's lean years,
a source of pride so sorely needed
a dedicated citizen devoted years
to the making of a model unlike any other,
half the size of the ship itself. Immense.

Skeptics might say the point of a model
was diminution, but never mind,
knock out the ceiling plaster, make room!
Up there, sheathed now under tarps,
the grand gesture sails nowhere still.

The building's scaffolded, closed—
not a moment too soon:
beautiful capitals peeled away
from their columns, the whole thing
sagged alarmingly to the left,

and we're lucky it becomes,
righted and redone, the new
Town Library. But not yet:
the headless steeple's crowned in blue,
plastic bandage to a strange wound . . .

My friends bought a place
on a sidestreet in a quiet part of town
once mostly Portuguese
though quickly gentrifying,
and set to work on renovations;

soft plaster replaced by Sheetrock,
floors sanded to a luster they maybe
never had, new wire strung
where the dangerous old knob
and tube had snaked for fifty years—

and that was just the main house.
Out back, beside the garden,
a derelict boathouse, capstone
of our tour, will be a studio;
blueprints show round windows,

French doors, a wedge of waterview.
Gutted now to the bare boards,
raised to pour a new foundation.
Simpler to start over, but town regs
say keep at least the walls

and you're safe from restrictions
meant to honor the historical.
Just this week excavations turned up
a clutch of antique bottles, shards of china,
and a human femur—

evidence of some old gravesite,
or a family burial plot, save
that it had been sawn neatly in half.
The contractor says don't tell a soul;
investigation could drag on

for months, who knows how deep
they'd want to dig? My friends say,
This stays here, in the garden,
and lift from scraggly peonies
sectioned segments of someone's thigh.

Half the town away, a peeled,
scumbling red: an old barn,
in my neighborhood, slated for demolition.
Until this year a sign sang on rusty hinges
CAPE COD SCHOOL OF THE ARTS,

and year after year the summer painters
trooped out with folding easels
for still lifes on the lawn
or portrait studies by the bay,
or scattered on the streets to paint

what charmed them. Out of earshot,
we'd laugh at their sweet renderings
of our garden gate, uniformly hued
as if some Impressionist Midas made
all he touched glow lavender and tangerine.

They learned from Henry Hensche
who painted here three-quarter century ago
when that barn was a rustic studio,
and local boys posed as fisherman or faun
while exiles from Boston hammered out

some path outside a bland American mainstream.
Their varnish dims, and distance gives
a strange stiff glamour, but something kindles
in those paintings still: authentic pulse
of an idiosyncratic flame. I was startled,

near sunset, when I first saw the shadows
in the sand *were* blued lavender,
and all the white houses on my block
were fired a subtle orange by the fierce
light-bending agency of the bay—

They were right, the Sunday painters,
but someone plans to raze
those high ceilings, north light,
my delicious boards—undertone
of vermilion, powdery

surface, burnished, varied, a shade
no one ever learned to mix
at the School of the Arts. You can't,
unless you have fifty years, and an exact
alchemy of brine air, sun, and fog.

When I say I hate time, Paul says
how else would we gain souls?
I don't want to agree, but then
I see the scoured, particular signature
of that red, the mortal push

that corrodes and rewrites.
Nothing makes the world more lovely.
I've done my share of fixing up;
I bought a house here, years ago,
stripped the place of shag and Formica,

shingled the roof in cedar shakes,
strove for a patina of age, planted old roses
and thrived on the equity.
Am I just one more crank
lamenting better, vanished days?

Just this morning, rounding the curve
near the saltmarsh,
we came upon a shocking pile—
that old restaurant that moldered there
for years, looking out over the moors,

with its fishnets and its glass globes,
beams hung with implements of the sea—
just a blare of wood and concrete now,
and soon to be—what else?—condos.
The new scours singularity away.

Weathering Heights, an empty nightclub
that brooded on a crest for years,
bulldozed—along with its dune—
to make room for a liquor store. Paul says,
There's renewal, and then there's murder.

Blanche Lazell's studio, Jo's waterfront Souvenirs
—which sold the same dozen things
three dozen years, and claimed, always,
a new shipment on the way—
scoured, knocked flat, torn down

to make way. Anthony Souza's place,
Anthony of the woolen army uniform
worn all seasons and weathers,
entirely deaf, deeply gregarious,
who lived seventy years in the mossy house

he was born in—now freshly turned out
in eggplant stain, roofed in copper,
with halogen lighting and a pond.
And Butchie's old place—
Butchie who used to wander the streets

in his glittery blue motorcycle helmet,
shirtless, belly domed and hard,
pulling a red wagon, saying salacious things
to tourists, and who one midnight stood
on the sidewalk holding a hapless turtle

he'd found, waving it in people's faces,
until a girl who worked at the pizza shop
and I bought it from him, because we knew
he'd drop it, and crack the captive's
mottled house apart—Butchie went

from the home to the grave;
his house scrubbed clean of him
and on the market. Well, what
do you want? Would you rather
the Methodist steeple tumbled down?

Which is worse, decay or restoration
that turns the past to a model of itself,
out of scale, new materials gleaming?
Should we save a rotting barn,
or a scatter of murderous evidence

turned up in the sand beneath
a sleek new studio? Who wouldn't want
such a lovely thing? Though it is, in fact,
a rental cottage, slipped past
the zoning laws to help with the mortgage

on the house. Quick, make it new,
before anyone finds the dirty evidence
of the bones. Anthony, Jo, Blanche Lazell:
we murder to renew. Won't time ruin
the boathouse rehab just as nicely?

This spring the weather's erratic,
chilly, dry; last winter it didn't snow at all.
The *Times* says in fifty years no more
coastal marshes, no more of the scent
on the air that indelible summer night,

fog-rubbed lights of the pizza parlor
starring out onto the street, and Butchie
weaving and carrying on. Nameless,
that midsummer marsh smell: acrid
and alive, equal parts fresh and curdling,

decay and setting out, shit and shinola.
Once it was a world without end,
dense with instruction in the arts
of revision and persistence,
that sharp salt-grass tang

inking the dark, while the town slept,
or some of it did. Odd sense of enchantment,
almost palpable. And Butchie was saying
to everyone, *Twenty bucks*
for a turtle. Who'd pay twenty bucks?

Heaven for Arden

Back when Arden could still go for a walk—a real walk,

not the twenty yards or so
he stumbles and lurches now—

he used to be anxious and uncertain, looking to me,

stopping awhile, tentatively, to see if I'd agree
to go no further, sometimes whining a bit

in case I'd respond. Sooner or later, the turn would come;

we'd gone far enough for one day. Joy!
As if he'd been afraid all along

this would be the one walk that would turn out to be infinite.

Then he could take comfort
in the certainty of an ending,

and treat the rest of the way as a series of possibilities;
then he could run,

and find pleasure in the woods beside the path.

Notes

HEAVEN FOR HELEN
For Helen Miranda Wilson.

FLIT
The black-capped chickadee, *Poecile atricapilla*.

HEAVEN FOR STANLEY
For Stanley Kunitz.

ULTRASOUND
Brenda Hillman: "The job of the living is to be seen through."

THE HOURS
After Michael Cunningham's novel, after Virginia Woolf.

NOTEBOOK/TO LUCIAN FREUD/ON THE VEIL
Italicized passages not otherwise credited are quotations from the painter found in William Feaver's *Lucian Freud*. The Melville quotation is from *Moby-Dick*, the Whitman from "Song of the Open Road."

IN THE SAME SPACE
Titled after Edmund Keeley and Philip Sherrard's translation of C. P. Cavafy's poem, which reads, in its entirety:

The setting of houses, cafés, the neighborhood
that I've seen and walked through years on end:

I created you while I was happy, while I was sad,
with so many incidents, so many details.

And, for me, the whole of you has been transformed into feeling.

SHAHID'S COUPLET

Remembers Agha Shahid Ali.

ONCOMING TRAIN

The italicized passage is from Andrew Marvell.

HEAVEN FOR PAUL

Paul: "What do you mean, *I* am the more nervous?"

Mark Twain: "The secret source of humor is not joy, but sorrow; there is no humor in heaven."

LETTER TO GOD

Based on a traditional story from Chiapas.

THE VAULT

The quotation from *The Gospel of Mary Magdalene* is translated by Jean-Yves Leloup and Joseph Rowe.

". . . when he was shown the most famous statues of Phidias and Glykon in order that he might use them as models, [Caravaggio's] only answer was to point towards a crowd of people, saying that nature had given him an abundance of masters."

G.P. Bellori, *Le vite de' pittori, scultori ed architecti moderni*, Rome, 1672, as translated in Howard Hibbard, *Caravaggio*, London, 1983

THE BLESSING

The opening line is derived from Stephen Mitchell's translation of Rilke's "Orpheus, Eurydice, Hermes."

FIRE TO FIRE

The italicized passage is from Whitman's "To You."

MEDITATION: "THE NIGHT OF TIME"

The final lines of the poem are after Gail Mazur.

Robinson Jeffers:
You, man and woman, live so long, it is hard
To think of you ever dying.
A little dog would get tired, living so long.

THE STAIRS

Homer:
. . . But when he knew he heard
Odysseus' voice nearby, he did his best
to wag his tail, nose down, with flattened ears,
having no strength to move nearer his master . . .

The Odyssey, translated by Robert Fitzgerald

PINK POPPY
    The Rilke quotation is from Stephen Mitchell's translation.

HEAVEN FOR BEAU
    May Swenson:
    How will I know
    in thicket ahead
    is danger or treasure
    when Body my good
    bright dog is dead . . .

TIME AND THE TOWN
    Borrows its title from Mary Heaton Vorse's memoir of
Provincetown life.

SCHOOL OF THE ARTS
    Blanche Lazell: pioneering Modernist printmaker whose
Provincetown studio was razed in 2001.

Abiding gratitude to Michael Carter and to Carol Muske Dukes for their
attentive, irreplaceable readings, to Lucie Brock-Broido, Marie Howe, Bill
Clegg, Terry Karten, Andrew Proctor, and Robin Robertson. And to Paul
Lisicky, above and beyond.